D1539354

Feng Shui for Dogs

Feng Shui
for Dogs

Illustrated by Chris Riddell

Text by Louise Howard

EBURY PRESS
LONDON

First published in 1997

9 10 8

First published in the United Kingdom in 1997 by Ebury Press
Random House · 20 Vauxhall Bridge Road · London SW1V 2SA

Random House Australia (Pty) Limited
20 Alfred Street · Milsons Point · Sydney · New South Wales 2061 · Australia

Random House New Zealand Limited
18 Poland Road · Glenfield · Auckland 10 · New Zealand

Random House South Africa (Pty) Limited
Endulini · 5a Jubilee Road · Parktown 2193 · South Africa

The Random House Group Limited Reg. No. 954009

www.randomhouse.co.uk

A CIP catalogue record for this book is available from the British Library

ISBN 0 09 186085 7

Designed by Martin Lovelock

Printed and bound in Great Britain by Mackays of Chatham plc, Kent

Contents

Chi

Chi is energy or force

If chi cannot flow through our legs, we are in trouble

Chi should flow upwards to the top of our heads

Bamboo flutes may help chi to flow

Electrical power can stimulate chi

Some people's chi repels us so we avoid them

Don't let your bed absorb negative chi

A confined space will debilitate your chi

A dilapidated dwelling kills chi

Protecting the chi of one's home
is a perpetual concern of Feng Shui

Harmony

If you balance your surroundings, you balance your self

Venerate the landscape

Yang is active

Yin is passive

Shapes have meaning ...

... and should balance

Focus clearly upon your needs ...

Then counterbalance them with your circumstances

Nature is perpetually in flux …

... yet cyclical

The size of door is all important

Bad door alignment can create division
between occupants

In some houses one feels happy and comfortable

In others one feels oppressed and ill at ease

Conscious intentions should cause harmony

Relationships

Analyse the clutter in your home and
compare it with your relationships

Clutter is an indication of troubled affairs

Clutter in the bed area may crowd out your love life

Try to let go of malign thoughts

Follow the natural rhythms of nature

Split levels may cause emotional disharmony

Balance and equilibrium restore
harmony between inhabitants

A split-level house can cause its occupants difficulty

Health

The quality of any water near you
is extremely important

54

Pieces of chalk in a little uncooked rice
placed beneath the bed can cure backache

Over-eating can be encouraged by hidden-away kitchens

Chopped-down trees may result in limb
or bone injury to residents

Avoid living near malign institutions,
such as funeral parlours

A difficult route to the bedroom may cause
a tendency to collapse on returning home

A door that opens the wrong way may cause
emotional anxiety

and even physical problems

A door at the end of a long narrow hall
may cause temperamental outbursts

You mirror your surroundings: if they are
in harmony, you will feel good too

A kitchen door that is too large
may cause an obsession with food

Oddly shaped gardens can be unsettling for residents

Oddly placed doors may result in unexpected calamities

Luck

Each dog starts out with good, medium or bad luck

Master connections and improve your fortune

Plants are auspicious and
can curb malign effects

If your lavatory is in the wealth area of your house
you may flush good fortune away

The shape of your bed can affect your luck

Find the best environment to live
up to your fullest potential

An auspiciously positioned desk
can increase prosperity

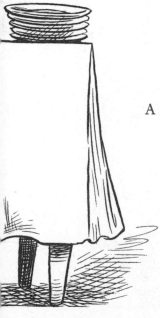

A mirror in the dining area attracts
money and therefore food

Send blessings to all corners of your home